Bibliographic information published by the German National Library:

The German National Library lists this publication in the National Bibliography; detailed bibliographic data are available on the Internet at http://dnb.dnb.de .

Imprint:

Copyright © 2018 GRIN Verlag
Print and binding: Books on Demand GmbH, Norderstedt Germany
ISBN: 9783346033543

This book at GRIN:

https://www.grin.com/document/499625

Theres Mitscherling

Deriving a big data analytics framework. Approaching the project management process for big data initiatives

A case study

GRIN Verlag

GRIN - Your knowledge has value

Since its foundation in 1998, GRIN has specialized in publishing academic texts by students, college teachers and other academics as e-book and printed book. The website www.grin.com is an ideal platform for presenting term papers, final papers, scientific essays, dissertations and specialist books.

Visit us on the internet:

http://www.grin.com/

http://www.facebook.com/grincom

http://www.twitter.com/grin_com

IFN702 – Demystifying the project management process for big data initiatives – A case study

Report

IFN 702 – Project 2

20f18 – Semester 2

Due 28-Oct-2018

Student Name: Theres Mitscherling

Contents

Abstract

This case study report investigated the project management approach for big data projects for industry partner Red Rocks Company. Big data is considered a key enabler for future decision making and process automation. The topic is however very new and not well understood yet. Hence 50% of big data projects are not delivering the expected benefits and are costing more than initially planned. Firstly, a brief literature review was undertaken to find out how big data projects are managed. From this, a Big Data Analytics Framework was derived which is based on CRISP-DM. As a second step, the framework was validated through interviews with stakeholders from the corporate sector. For this case study, the first three phases of the Business Process Management Lifecycle were applied: process discovery, analysis and design. Key findings of the case study are that literature recommends an agile project management approach for big data initiatives. On the contrary, the majority of interviewed industry stakeholders confirmed a waterfall approach is conducted more often to deliver such projects. The developed Big Data Analytics Framework was validated and will add significant benefits to Red Rocks Company as it will help to successfully deliver big data initiatives in future.

A. Introduction

Background

Big data has been a topic of high attention for organisations in the past 10 years. Heudecker defines big data as "high volume, velocity and/or variety information assets that demand cost-effective, innovative forms of information processing that enable enhanced insight, decision making, and process automation" (2013, p. 2). A recent study confirmed that 82% of organizations believe that big data gives them a competitive advantage in today's fast-paced business environment (Vanson Bourne. 2015). In a global and highly-connected world, it enables organizations to identify patterns and to make smart business decisions based on facts delivered by big data platforms. However, 50% of organisations state that big data initiatives have been more expensive than originally expected (Hendershot. 2016). The reason for this is that the topic is rather new and not very well understood, therefore big data initiatives are often underestimated and are not returning the expected benefits to organisations.

The aim of this project is to understand best practice project management for big data initiatives and to develop a framework to help such projects to deliver the expected advantages.

Industry partner

With over 53,000 employees, the Red Rocks Company is one of the largest global mining operators with mines in Australia, Chile, the USA and many other countries. The organisation's technology vision is "to enable a fully integrated and highly automated business from resource to market by 2025" (Red Rocks Company. 2018). Big data is a fundamental building block to achieve a "fully integrated business".

Red Rocks Company is in the process of establishing a big data platform which will be used by at least 12 different customers (mine sites). There is limited expertise in this area of the business and therefore the organization is seeking to understand what the challenges and considerations in managing big data initiatives are and the associated best practice project management.

Project objective

This project seeks to understand best practice project management for big data initiatives. Firstly, it will undertake a preliminary literature review to derive a framework for managing big data initiatives. Secondly, it will validate the framework by undertaking interviews with project team members, internal and external to industry partner Red Rocks Company, that have been involved in successful Big data projects within the corporate sector. Audience of this work are industry partners and academic researchers in the big data discipline.

Significance

Big data is a growing area into which organisations are investing to develop capabilities. The project will deliver significant research for practitioners and researchers due to the novel nature of the topic. It will provide insights into how to manage big data projects which will help the Red Rocks company to achieve the 2025 vision of "highly integrated and fully automated".

B. Research methodology

Business Process Management Lifecycle

The project predominantly followed the Business Process Management (BPM) Lifecycle as per Dumas (2016) to develop a standardised process. The aim of this model is to improve the performance of a process. The BPM Lifecycle is structured into five phases (see **Figure 1 - The BPM Lifecycle model (Dumas. 2016)**) and provides a simple and easy to follow structure to achieve continuous improvement in Business Process Management.

This model was selected because it is considered industry best practice (Bernado et al. 2017) and it aligns with methodologies currently applied within Red Rocks Company.

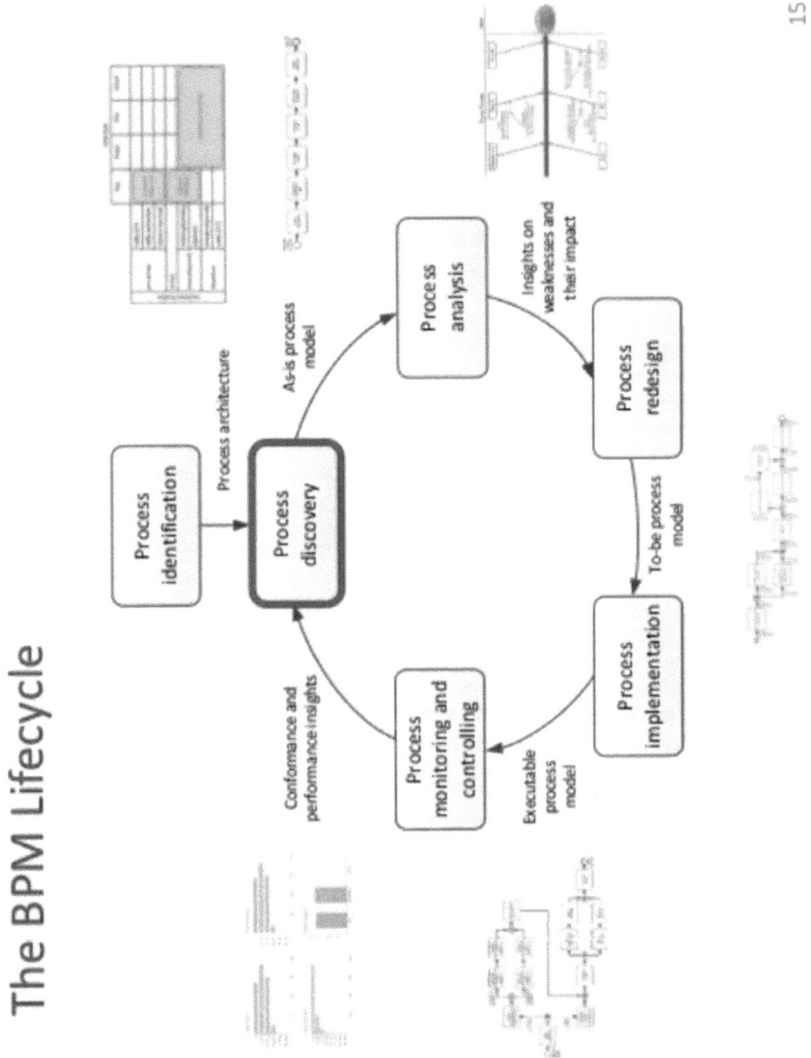

Figure 1 - The BPM Lifecycle model (Dumas. 2016)

This process was identified and requested to be reviewed by one of the key stakeholders of Red Rocks Company as part of this work. As part of the project discovery and analysis, a literature review and interviews were undertaken. An outcome of the review was the development of this new framework which fits into the process redesign phase of the BPM Lifecycle model.

For this project, only the first three of the five phases are in scope (see **Figure 2 - In scope phases for this project as per BPM Lifecycle**). This is mainly due to the project execution time of 12 weeks which is too restrictive to implement a new process in a large organisation like Red Rocks Company and to receive performance insights via a feedback loop. Perhaps this will be part of a follow-on project.

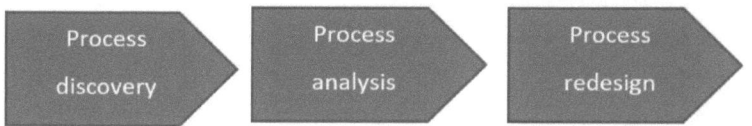

Figure 2 - In scope phases for this project as per BPM Lifecycle model

Method overview

A combination of methods was applied in this project. Initially, a brief literature review was undertaken from which a Big Data Analytics Framework was derived. This was then validated through interviews.

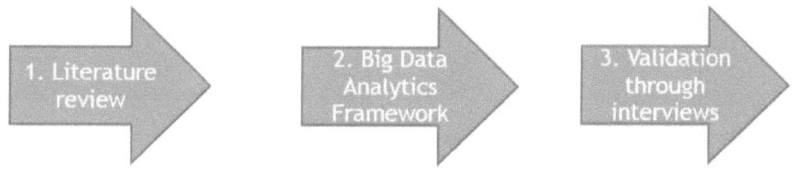

Figure 3 - Method overview

Literature review

The project undertook a brief literature review of nine artefacts, which adopted the guidelines by Bandara et al (2015). Reason for choosing these guidelines is that they provide a validated framework within academia.

Phase 1 - Extraction of literature

The first phase is the extraction of literature. An online search was conducted in the QUT library and Google Scholar to find relevant literature. The reason for using both libraries was to ensure no important articles were missed. Google Scholar is an online search engine for academic publications. It was not used before by the author and there was a certain curiosity to see the difference in search results. The Gartner, Project Management Institute (PMI) and McKinsey databases were also searched for industry-relevant literature that was not available in the QUT library or Google Scholar. The following search word parameters were used:

- Big data and project management
- Big data and project management approach

An initial search presented the following results as in the table below. The relevant articles were then coded using the top 3 main ideas.

Search word combination	QUT library	Google scholar
"Big data" and "project management"	743,448	3,560,000
"Big data" and "project management approach"	235,357	593,000

Table 1 - Literature review search results

Phase 2 – Organization and preparation for analysis of artefacts

The top documents from each search were reviewed and categorized in the below table. Initially the abstract was reviewed for relevant paragraphs to "big data" and "project management". All reviewed artefacts had some content on big data but not all presented insights on the project management approach. The top 3 main ideas were noted in the coding table for each article. Early on there was a trend identified that big data projects are suited to an agile project management approach and that CRISP-DM is a foundational process. Therefore two additional criterion were added to the evaluation table to mark the articles that supported this idea. The criteria used for literature review success:

- Contains relevant information and insights on Big data projects
- Contains information on the project management approach
- Classified by the article supporting the idea of using an agile approach for Big data projects

The literature analysis was kept to9 articles that contain valuable content to the research topic. Other artefacts were reviewed by reading the abstract, however, most of the content addressed the theme at a very high level and did not add new knowledge. Further, contemporary articles were chosen from different industries to ensure good questionnaire design.

Phase 3 – Coding and analysis

An initial coding and analysis was undertaken as per table below. The data were classified into the title, source, author, published year and top 3 main ideas. Two classifiers were established to note if the article supported the idea that an agile approach is suited for big data projects and the CRISP-DM process.

# Title	Source	Author	Year	Agile approach	CRISP DM applied	Main idea #1	Main idea #2	Main idea #3
1 <Title>	<Library source>	<Author>	<YYYY>	Yes / No	Yes / No	<Main idea #x in form of a quote or summarized in own words>		
2								

Table 2 - Literature review coding and analysis table

The coding and analysis were undertaken in Microsoft Excel and can be found in Appendix 2 – Literature review details.

Phase 4 – Write up and presentation

This phase was undertaken as part of Section C - Results.

Interviews

Interviews was selected as a method to validate the Big Data Analytics Framework. Validation of theoretical models is of significant importance, because it proves that the model is sound and it is required for the ongoing application (MacKenzie et al, 2011). Interviews provided objective answers to validate the framework in such a short period of time. A survey with a questionnaire would have been too subjective. A questionnaire was developed based on the literature review and stakeholder input. It can be found in **Appendix 4 - Questionnaire**. The questionnaire had eight focus areas:

1. Confirm the size and complexity of the big data environment to enable comparison
2. The initial goal of the big data project to be able to categorise into operational or innovative nature
3. Discovery steps undertaken
4. Project management methodology used
5. Challenges encountered
6. Benefits derived
7. Stakeholder management
8. Application of the CRISP-DM framework.

8

Five face to face interviews were held at Red Rocks Company and outside over a two month timeframe in Brisbane, Australia. Interviews were recorded and later transcribed for research purposes. From the limited interviewees, a number of disciplines were interviewed including senior project managers, technical infrastructure staff and data scientists. All interviews related to big data projects in the corporate sector and had a varied duration of 7-30 min.

Interview #	Industry	Date	Appendix
#1	Finance	09-Sep-2018	Appendix 5 – Transcript interview 1
#2	Mining	14-Sep-2018	Appendix 6 – Transcript interview 2
#3	Oil & Gas	26-Sep-2018	Appendix 7 – Transcript interview 3
#4	Mining	26-Sep-2018	Appendix 8 – Transcript interview 4
#5	Mining	09-Oct-2018	Appendix 9 – Transcript interview 5

Table 3 - Summary of interviews

Project management approach for this research project

Scrum is an agile project management framework that was selected for this project. Schwaber et al (2017, p. 3) defines Scrum as "a framework within which people can address complex adaptive problems, while productively and creatively delivering products of the highest possible value". There were be five sprints of equal duration of two weeks over the course of the project. A product backlog was established to manage the requirements of the project.

Sprint #1		Sprint #2		Sprint #3		Sprint #4			Sprint #5	
Week 3	Week 4	Week 5	Week 6	Week 7	Week 8	Week 9	Week 10	Week 11	Week 12	
Presentation	M1 - Project plan	M2 – Literature review final			M5 - Surveys and interviews				M6 – Presentation	
	Literature review #1	Draft framework		M3 - Finalize questionnaire			Analyse responses	Draft final report	M7 - Submit the report	
	Questionnaire draft			M4 - Review framework						

Figure 4 - Sprint and task breakdown overview

Key deliverables of this project include:

- Brief literature review
- Big data Analytics framework
- Validation through interviews:
  - Questionnaire
  - Interviews and transcripts
- Case study report to present findings.

The main reason for selecting Scrum for this project is that it is simple to understand and provides an early feedback mechanism for stakeholders which is important for the success of the project. Hotle (2017) states that early stakeholder feedback is one of the key benefits of a Scrum agile approach.

C. Results

Summary of literature review results

Nine artefacts were reviewed in the initial literature review. From this selection, five articles confirmed that agile is the recommended project management approach for big data projects, one referred to a waterfall based approach and three had no information to confirm the project management approach. Although there was no evidence on the project management approach for three reviews, they were still listed as they contained important insights into the significance of big data initiatives.

#	Literature title	Big data projects are suited to be managed using an agile approach
1	Using agile to accelerate your data transformation	Yes
2	Agile project management approach and its use in big data management	Yes
3	Data done right	No, nil on PM approach
4	How to Operationalize Machine Learning and Data Science Projects	No, nil on PM approach
5	Managing a Big data project: The case of Ramco Cements Limited	No, waterfall
6	Six Pitfalls to Avoid When Planning Data Science and Machine Learning Projects	Yes
7	Drive Analytics Innovation by Using a Bimodal Approach	Yes
8	Big data and the Internet of Things Enterprise Information Architecture for a New Age	Yes
9	Big data Computing : A Guide for Business and Technology Managers	No, nil on PM approach

Table 4 - Literature review results

Two out of the nine kinds of literatures were case studies and provided contradicting recommendations. Frankova et al (2016) undertook a survey with conference participants which determined that agile is the preferred approach for big data projects. The article concludes that it is recommended to start with a small use case, learn from failures and continue with an iterative approach. On the contrary, Dutta et al (2015) suggests using a waterfall approach with a thoroughly planned project plan to ensure successful execution, deployment and acceptance by the end users. This is validated with that big data projects are new to most organisations and more difficult to implement. Big data projects require significant change management to adjust the mindset of users by making decisions based on the data provided instead of intuition.

The differentiating industries from which the case studies were understood, could be the reason for the contrary opinions. The work undertaken by Frankova et al was based on a survey at a conference, whereas Dutta's was established on a case study that implemented a big data solution at a cement manufacturer which is culturally close to the resources sector in which Red Rocks Company operates. This may lead to the conclusion that the primary resources sector is more aligned to a waterfall project management approach due to the industry's nature of establishing large, complex and long living assets like mine sites and plants. There was no evidence found to support this conclusion in the literature and further research into this particular topic may be required outside of this work.

Waterfall approach

The waterfall model is the traditional project management approach which uses a sequential design flow. First applied as far back as the 1950s, it is still popular for engineering and construction projects. The Ramco case study (Dutta et al. 2015) confirmed that waterfall is a recommended approach for big data analytics projects. Further, the majority of interviews followed this approach. It was noted that the industry background of the case study and also the interviews is resourcing in form of mining or oil & gas.

Agile

The Agile Manifesto was first defined in 2001 by a group of independent software developers (Schneider. 2017). As per Schneider (2017, p. 2), the Agile mindset is all about building the right solution today and acknowledging that this might not be the right solution tomorrow. Compared to the waterfall approach, it is rapid and iterative. Agile focuses on quality whilst applying continuous improvement principles. The literature review identified that the vast majority of sighted artefacts recommended an agile project management approach for big data analytics projects. On the contrary, only one interview confirmed this and another interview stated that a hybrid approach of waterfall and agile was applied.

CRISP-DM

The Cross-Industry Process for Data Mining, also referred to as CRISP-DM, was first defined by a group of data scientists in 1999 (Chapman et al, 1999). Although not a project management methodology, it is a data analysis process that provides the basis for a significant number of data analytics frameworks

12

that are known today. The initial literature review did not recognise CRISP-DM as a process for big data projects. One of the interviewees uses the approach and two other interviews confirmed, that although officially a waterfall approach was used, intuitively CRIPS-DM was applied. An additional literature review confirmed, that CRISP DM provides the fundamentals behind successful data analytics projects up until today (Mariscal et al, 2010).

Hybrid agile and waterfall approach

Hayata et al (2011) states that a hybrid agile and waterfall approach is an evolving trend within organisations. Organisational change takes time and as technology teams are accustomed to their traditional way of working in a waterfall approach, the transition to an agile organisation can take many years. By using an agile and waterfall approach, it allows the organization to practice some of the agile techniques while remaining in waterfall-based world (Hotle et al, 2018). The initial literature review did not find supporting evidence for a hybrid agile and waterfall project management approach. The majority of the documents were very clear to validate an agile approach. However, the interviews confirmed that a hybrid approach was used although sometimes not prescribed and rather unknowingly. Two of the interviews operated in a waterfall approach. However, when questioned on the techniques and processes like CRISP DM used for the data analytics, it was confirmed that unknowingly this process has been followed. Further, interview 1 used a very pure agile approach which enabled the team to quickly commission a working solution to the organisation. Although one of the challenges encountered was insufficient licensing which could have been prevented by using a traditional waterfall approach. This suggests that a hybrid agile and waterfall approach would be more suitable for this organisation.

Summary of interview findings

The results of the interviews are rather broad. A correlation between projects of operational character (i.e. development of Spotfire report for operational data) and applying a waterfall project management approach is evident. Further, projects that followed an agile or hybrid agile waterfall approach had a more innovative and incubator character (i.e. predictive maintenance data analytics). Projects that were delivered in a waterfall approach still initiated a constant feedback loop with the customer, which is indicative for an agile approach. This leads us to assume that project personnel are intuitively seeking constant stakeholder feedback to ensure the success of the project although not prescribed in the waterfall approach. Overall, the majority of the individual steps of the Big Data Analytics Framework were validated during the interviews.

#	Category	Interview #1	Interview #2	Interview #3	Interview #4	Interview #5
1	Size	Medium	Large	Small	Small	Small
2	Industry	Finance	Mining	Oil & Gas	Mining	Mining
3	Project management approach	Agile	Waterfall + Agile	Waterfall	Waterfall	Waterfall
4	Project type	Innovation	Innovation	Operational	Operational	Operational
5	CRISP-DM	No	Yes	No, but intuitively used	No, but intuitively used	No
6	Key step: Understand & Prepare data	No	Yes	Yes	Yes	No

Table 5 - Interview findings

Big data Analytics Framework

The below Big Data Analytics Framework has been derived from the findings of the literature review and interviews as a suitable approach for the Red Rocks Company to undertake big data projects. The framework has seven steps and is based on a hybrid agile and waterfall approach. The foundations of the approach are based on CRISP-DM.

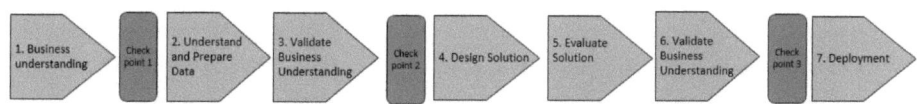

Figure 5- Big Data Analytics Framework

1. Business Understanding

"Business Understanding" is the first step of the Business Data Analytics Framework. The key goal of this phase is to understand the objectives of the project and business requirements. This is also the phase where the current AS IS status is determined, including an inventory of resources. The interviews confirmed that business understanding is critical. Especially interview 5 highlighted that "creating a gap analysis to help understand the business" was important for success. Brocchi et al (2016) state that a business-driven approach is one of the core principals of any digital

14

transformation. Under this model, organisations create use cases and requirements whilst taking inventory of data associations for different use cases and opportunities. This step is followed by "Checkpoint 1" to determine if the initiative is still to progress or needs to be reprioritised. It is proceeded by step "2. Understand and Prepare Data".

The business understanding is validated again in step 3 and 6 of the process to confirm that original requirements and objectives are still valid. The reason for repeating this step is that it is crucial to understand the customer's expectation on the big data initiative.

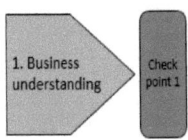

Figure 6 - Big Data Analytics Framework - 1. Business Understanding

2. Understand and Prepare Data

"Understand and Prepare Data" is the second step of the Big data Analytics Framework. This is the phase where data is collected, explored, cleansed and formatted. Interview 4 confirmed that this stage is often used for a Proof of Concept (PoC) which may aide in realising the idea and providing more data insights. Bocchi et al (2016) also state that pilot projects in form of minimum viable products can help the organisation to understand their available data better and therefore accelerate the successful delivery of the project. The benefit is that a small solution is developed and validated with the customer before extensive development effort is spent on the final solution. Further, Interview 2 discussed the work to discover all the data but an even larger effort in mapping the data which took 1 year of discovery for a single data set. Undertaking this step built the foundation for the successful implementation of the solution. Henderson (2016, p. 5) states that "in order to be useful, data needs to be contextualized and cleansed and brought into the context where each stakeholder lives", which highlights the importance of this phase. This is followed by "3. Validate Business Understanding".

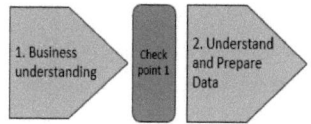

Figure 7 - Big Data Analytics Framework - 2. Understand and Prepare Data

3. Validate Business Understanding

"Validate Business Understanding" is the third step of the Business Data Analytics Framework. The purpose of this step is to validate the initial project objective and customer requirements from step 1 and to re-prioritise against competing initiatives. It is an opportunity for the business to stop the project or slow down the process. Chapman et al (1999) confirm that big data analysis is not a rigid process and requires constant going back and forth between the phases. This step is followed by "Checkpoint 2" to determine if the initiative is still to progress or needs to be reprioritised. It is followed by step 4, "Design Solution".

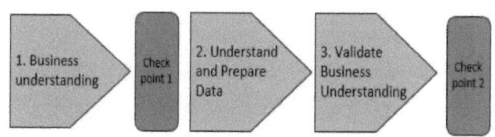

Figure 8 - Big Data Analytics Framework - 3. Validate Business Understanding

4. Design Solution

"Design Solution" is the fourth step of the Business Data Analytics Framework. Purpose of this step is to build the data model using selected techniques and to develop a test plan (Chapman et al, 1999). Interviews 3 and 4 confirmed that this step requires the necessary pre-work in order to be successful. This step is followed by "5. Evaluate Solution".

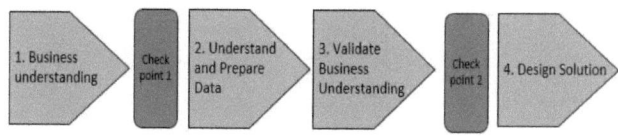

Figure 9 - Big Data Analytics Framework - 4. Design Solution

5. Evaluate Solution

"Evaluate Solution" is the fifth step of the Business Data Analytics Framework. Purpose of this step is to undertake a technical evaluation of the model before implementing it. This is where data results are evaluated and the process is reviewed (Chapman et al, 1999). As stated in interview 1, evaluating the solution before deploying it is critical to ensure no key processes are overlooked. This is followed by step 6, "Validate Business Understanding".

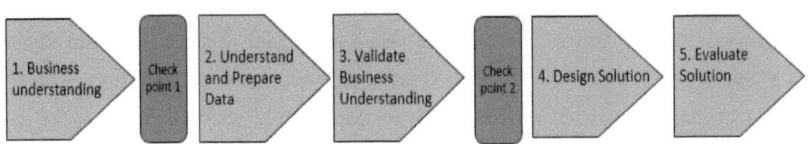

Figure 10 - Big Data Analytics Framework - 5. Evaluate Solution

6. Validate Business Understanding

"Validate Business Understanding" is the sixth step of the Business Data Analytics Framework. It is a repetition of step 3, however, the initiative has now matured. The purpose of this stage is to review the initial project objectives and requirements identified in step 1 (Chapman et al, 1999). It is the final validation step before the solution is deployed. As stated in interview 2, big data analytics is a constant discovery and validation of business understanding. Interview 3 also applied a constant feedback loop.

This step is followed by "Checkpoint 3" to determine if the initiative is still to progress or needs to be reprioritised. It is proceeded by step 7, "Deployment".

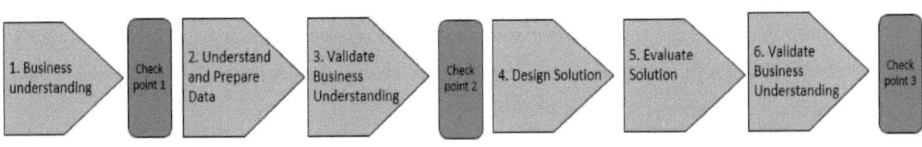

Figure 11 - Big Data Analytics Framework - 6. Validate Business Understanding

7. Deployment

"Deployment" is the seventh step of the Business Analytics Framework. This is the stage when the deployment plan is executed and a final project report/review is produced (Chapman et al, 1999). It is the final step of the process.

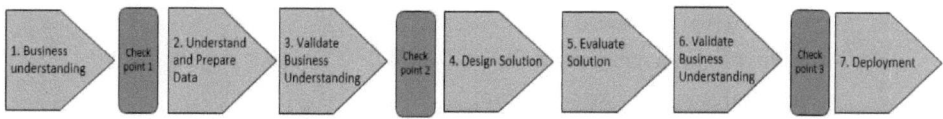

Figure 12 - Big Data Analytics Framework - 7. Deployment

D. Discussion

The key motivation for this work was to identify best project management practices that will help Red Rocks Company to deliver big data initiatives successfully. The initial aim of the project has been met. Whilst the Big data Analytics Framework has not been validated yet in practice, it provides a strong foundation for the future to improve the current failure rate of 50% (Hendershot. 2016). Further, it will help organisations to realize the benefits of their big data initiatives by enabling smart business decision making based on facts and automation. The work identified various findings related to big data analytics initiatives which were derived from the literature review and interviews, and can be viewed in below table.

#	Component	Evidence in interviews	Evidence in the literature
1	Literature review suggests that an agile project management approach is the recommended project management method for big data.	No	Yes
2	Interview findings are suggesting that the waterfall project management approach is the recommended project management method for big data.	Yes	No
3	The resource industry prefers a waterfall approach to agile.	Yes	No
4	Big data Analytics projects require strong stakeholder engagement.	Yes	Yes
5	CRISP-DM forms the foundation for successful big data analytics projects.	Yes	Yes
6	Big data analytics requires an iterative approach in order to be successful.	Yes	Yes

Table 6 – Summary of findings

While this case study introduces a Big Data Analytics Framework, it has only been validated by literature and interviews of this research project. Some of the limitations include the number of interviews held (five) and level of interviewee maturity which ranged from technical staff to senior project managers. Further, measurable improvements can only be determined after process implementation which was not in the scope of this project. Additional research is required to validate the aforementioned limitations and the Big Data Analytics Framework.

E. Conclusion

Big data Analytics is a key enabler for organisations to stay competitive in fast-paced markets. About 50% of organisations state that their big data analytics projects did not return the expected benefits and ended up costing more than initially expected. Further, there is currently very limited research on how to manage big data projects successfully. The Big Data Analytics Framework introduced in this case study has been found to be a valuable process for managing such initiatives successfully. Firstly, a literature review was undertaken to identify common trends in big data projects. Secondly, the Big Data Analytics Framework was developed using the aforementioned learnings. Thirdly, interviews were undertaken to validate the new process. The case study found that although an agile project management is the recommended method for such projects as per the literature review, the interviews did not confirm this in practice. Further, CRISP-DM is still the foundation for a lot of big data frameworks and also forms the basis for the Big Data Analytics Framework introduced in this work. The framework will provide Red Rocks Company with a valuable tool to engage successfully in their big data journey.

The findings of this work could be limited by the number of interviews held and the level of maturity of the interviewees. Additionally, measurable improvements can only be determined after the implementation, which was out of scope for this case study project. The findings reflect what was initially expected. Further research is required to validate the Big Data Analytics framework as a whole after process implementation.

Abbreviations

BPM	Business Process Management
CRISP-DM	Cross-Industry Process for Data Mining
PoC	Proof of Concept

References

Bandara, Wasana et al (2015). Achieving Rigor in Literature Reviews: Insights from Qualitative Data Analysis and Tool Support.

Bernardo, R., Galina, S. V. R., & Pádua, S. I.,Dallavalle de. (2017). The BPM lifecycle. Business Process Management Journal, 23(1), 155-175.

Brocci et al (2016). Using agile to accelerate your data transformation. Retrieved on Aug 8, 2018 from https://www.mckinsey.com/business-functions/digital-mckinsey/our-insights/using-agile-to-accelerate-your-data-transformation.

Chapman et al (1999). CRISP-DM 1.0. Retrieved on Sep 27, 2018 from ftp://ftp.software.ibm.com/software/analytics/spss/support/Modeler/Documentation/14/UserManual/CRISP-DM.pdf.

Dumas, M. (2016). BPM Techniques and Tools: A Quick Tour of the BPM Lifecycle. Retrieved on Mar 15, 2018 from https://www.slideshare.net/MarlonDumas/bpm-techniques-and-tools-a-quick-tour-of-the-bpm-lifecycle.

Dutta, D., & Bose, I. (2015). Managing a Big data project: The case of Ramco Cements Limited. International Journal of Production Economics, 165, 293–306. doi:10.1016/j.ijpe.2014.12.032

Hayata, T., & Han, J. (n.d.). A hybrid model for IT project with Scrum. Service Operations, Logistics, and Informatics (SOLI), 2011 IEEE International Conference on (pp. 285–290). IEEE Publishing. doi:10.1109/SOLI.2011.5986572.

Hendershot, S. (2016). Data done right: learning to target the right type of data can uncover insights that drive project success. PM Network, 30(3), 40–45.

Heudecker, N. (2013). Hype Cycle for Big data 2013. Retrieved on Aug 16, 2018 from https://www.gartner.com/document/code/252431?ref=grbody&refval=2589121.

Hotle, M., & Wilson, N. (2018). Move Away From Waterfall to Agile and Product-Centric Delivery Methods. Retrieved on Sep-30, 2018 from